Gymnastics

by Jill Sherman

BELLWETHER MEDIA • MINNEAPOLIS, MN

Note to Librarians, Teachers, and Parents:

Blastoff! Readers are carefully developed by literacy experts and combine standards-based content with developmentally appropriate text.

Level 1 provides the most support through repetition of high-frequency words, light text, predictable sentence patterns, and strong visual support.

Level 2 offers early readers a bit more challenge through varied simple sentences, increased text load, and less repetition of high-frequency words.

Level 3 advances early-fluent readers toward fluency through increased text and concept load, less reliance on visuals, longer sentences, and more literary language.

Level 4 builds reading stamina by providing more text per page, increased use of punctuation, greater variation in sentence patterns, and increasingly challenging vocabulary.

Level 5 encourages children to move from "learning to read" to "reading to learn" by providing even more text, varied writing styles, and less familiar topics.

Whichever book is right for your reader, Blastoff! Readers are the perfect books to build confidence and encourage a love of reading that will last a lifetime!

This edition first published in 2020 by Bellwether Media, Inc.

No part of this publication may be reproduced in whole or in part without written permission of the publisher. For information regarding permission, write to Bellwether Media, Inc., Attention: Permissions Department, 6012 Blue Circle Drive, Minnetonka, MN 55343.

Library of Congress Cataloging-in-Publication Data

Names: Sherman, Jill, author.
Title: Gymnastics / by Jill Sherman.
Description: Minneapolis, MN : Bellwether Media, Inc., 2020. | Series: Blastoff! Readers : Let's Play Sports! | Includes bibliographical references and index. | Audience: Ages: 5-8. | Audience: Grades: K-3.
Identifiers: LCCN 2018058477 (print) | LCCN 2019003012 (ebook) | ISBN 9781618915412 (ebook) | ISBN 9781644870006 (hardcover : alk. paper)
Subjects: LCSH: Gymnastics–Juvenile literature.
Classification: LCC GV461.3 (ebook) | LCC GV461.3 .S44 2020 (print) | DDC 796.44–dc23
LC record available at https://lccn.loc.gov/2018058477

Editor: Rebecca Sabelko   Designer: Andrea Schneider

Printed in the United States of America, North Mankato, MN.

Table of Contents

What Is Gymnastics?

Gymnastics is a sport that tests **flexibility,** strength, and **balance**.

Gymnasts complete **routines** at gyms. They do their routines alone. But they are sometimes scored as a team.

flexibility

routine

Gymnastics is popular all over the world!

2016 Summer Olympics in Brazil

Simone Biles

- **USA National Team**
- **Artistic gymnastics**
- **Accomplishments:**
  - **5 Olympic medals:**
    4 gold
    1 bronze
  - **14 world championship medals:**
    10 gold
    2 silver
    2 bronze

Most people watch the sport during the **Olympics**.

vault

Gymnastics includes many events. **Floor exercise** and **vault** are popular.

Gymnasts use moves like **cartwheels** and **handsprings**. These moves are used together in routines.

handspring

Men and women often **compete** in different events. Men whip their legs around **pommel horses**. Women dance on balance beams.

balance beam

Gymnastics Events

Men's Events

floor exercise

horizontal bar

vault

still rings

pommel horse

parallel bars

Women's Events

floor exercise

vault

balance beam

uneven bars

Two sets of judges score routines. One looks at the **difficulty** of routines. The other watches for mistakes.

Gymnasts push themselves to earn a perfect score!

still rings

judge

floor exercise

13

In many competitions, gymnasts begin with a 10.0 score. Judges remove points for mistakes.

uneven
bars

Points are removed for many reasons. Gymnasts can lose points for losing their balance or not pointing their toes.

Gymnastics Gear

leotard

Gymnasts wear **leotards**.
Men may wear pants as well.

The tight clothing lets judges see each gymnast's form.

pommel horse

17

Swinging on bars and rings requires a good grip. Gymnasts use chalk to keep from slipping.

grips

GYMNASTICS GEAR

leotard

grips

chalk

Some gymnasts wear
special leather **grips**.

19

Mats are important in all events. They soften landings and falls.

Every routine is a challenge. Gymnasts are always putting their bodies to the test!

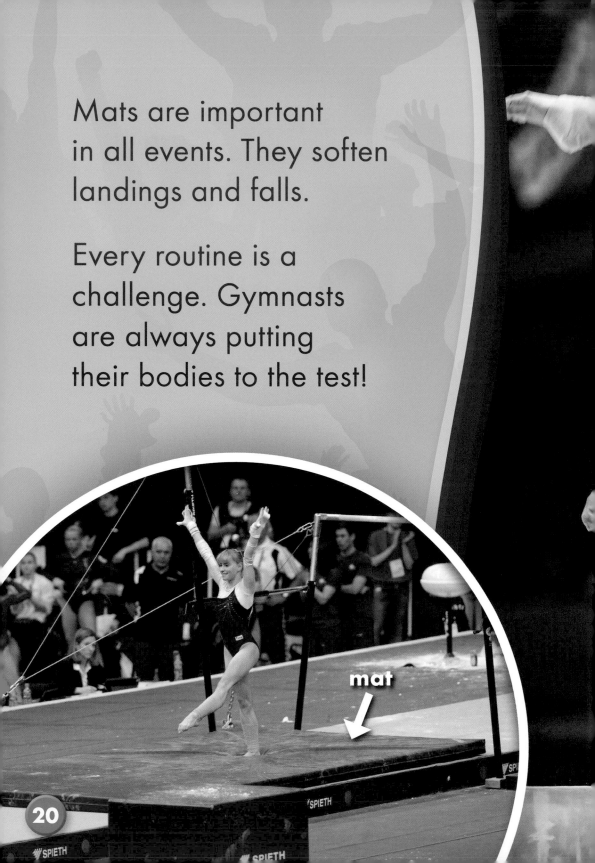

mat

Glossary

balance—moving or staying in the same place without losing control or falling

cartwheels—a sideways movement done by placing one hand and then the other on the ground, before lifting the feet into the air and landing on one foot before the other

compete—to try to win something someone else is also trying to win

difficulty—how hard it is to do something

flexibility—the ability to move and bend easily

floor exercise—a gymnastics event in which a gymnast performs a routine including dance, jumps, and other movements

grips—leather straps that keep gymnasts' hands safe

handsprings—movements in which a gymnast turns the body in a full circle from a standing position and lands first on the hands and then on the feet

leotards—stretchy, tight uniforms worn by gymnasts

Olympics—short for the Olympic Games; the Olympic Games are worldwide summer or winter sports contests held in a different country every four years.

pommel horses—thick benches with two handles on top of the benches

routines—actions gymnasts follow for a performance

vault—a gymnastics event in which gymnasts leap over a form

To Learn More

Murray, Julie. *Gymnastics*. Minneapolis, Minn.: Abdo Kids, 2018.

Rebman, Nick. *Gymnastics*. Lake Elmo, Minn.: Focus Readers, 2019.

Sherman, Jill. *Cheerleading*. Minneapolis, Minn.: Bellwether Media, 2020.

ON THE WEB

Factsurfer.com gives you a safe, fun way to find more information.

1. Go to www.factsurfer.com.

2. Enter "gymnastics" into the search box and click 🔍.

3. Select your book cover to see a list of related web sites.

Index

The images in this book are reproduced through the courtesy of: Jiang Dao Hua, front cover (gymnast); Polhansen, front cover (gym); Just dance, pp. 4 (inset), 16-17 (top); Leonard Zhukovsky, pp. 4-5; 506 collection/ Alamy, pp. 6-7 (bottom); Petr Toman, p. 7 (Simone Biles); Sasha Samardzija, pp. 6-7 (top), 9 (bottom); Chris Van Lennep, p. 10; Echo/ Getty, p. 12 (inset); A.RICARDO, pp. 12-13; Aspen Photos, p. 14 (bottom); Kyodo News/ Getty, pp. 14-15 (top); Master1305, p. 17 (bottom); sportpoint, pp. 18, 19 (grips); 695362087, p. 19 (leotard); PCN Photography/ Alamy, p. 19 (chalk); ID1974, p. 20 (inset); NurPhoto/ Getty Images, pp. 20-21.